Chung · Hyo · Ye

Tales of filial devotion, loyalty, respect and benevolence from the history and folklore of Korea

Front cover: image of a heavenly being offering an incense burner to the Buddha.
Taken from the Sacred Bell of King Songdok (cast AD 771),
"the world's most beautiful bell" in the view of many scholars and artists worldwide.

Edited by
Diamond Sutra Recitation Group

Yong Hwa Publications
1269 Seonggokri Heunghae Bukgu
Pohang, Korea

First edition, April 2007
Second edition, December 2007

ISBN: 0-9779613-9-7

Printed in the Republic of Korea

This book is dedicated to Anne, Sandy, Joanne, Amber-Leigh Christine, Shawn, Eric, and Amy. Without their help and support, this book couldn't have been written.

—Jim Keogh, MSN, RN-BC

About the Author

Jim Keogh, MSN, RN-BC, is Board Certified in Psychiatric-Mental Health and has written McGraw-Hill's *Nursing Demystified* series. These include *Pharmacology Demystified, Microbiology Demystified, Medical-Surgical Nursing Demystified, Medical Billing and Coding Demystified, Nursing Laboratory and Diagnostic Tests Demystified, Dosage Calculations Demystified, Medical Charting Demystified, Pediatric Nursing Demystified, Nurse Management Demystified, Schaum's Outline of ECG Interpretations, Schaum's Outline of Medical Terminology*, and *Schaum's Outline of Emergency Nursing*. His books can be found in leading university libraries, including Yale School of Medicine, Yale University, University of Pennsylvania Biomedical Library, Columbia University, Brown University, University of Medicine and Dentistry of New Jersey, Cambridge University, and Oxford University. He is a former member of the faculty at Columbia University and is a member of the faculty of New York University and Saint Peter's University in New Jersey.

Transport, energy consumption and, 16–17
Trees, *See* Forestry; Timber
Trellis-climbing plants, 162–3
Trief-cement, 96
Trinidad asphalt, 144
Tropical timber, 159–61
Tunnel kilns, 134
Turbulence membranes, 254
Turf, 161–2
  roofs, 328–37
Turpentine, 406

Under-developed countries, 15
Underground buildings, 272–4
Unused resources, 5, 6–7
Usable resources, 3
Used resources, 5

Vapour barriers, 250
Vapour permeability, 60
Varnish, 401–3
Vermiculite, 91, 266–7
Vinyl floor coverings, 363
Vitrifying kilns, 136

Wallpapers, 366–73
  history, 367–8
  types of, 368–73
Walls:
  breathing, 255
  cavity walls, 253
  dry-stone walling, 202
  peat, 237
  timber, 231–4
  See also Cladding
Warmth-reflecting materials, 247–8
Waste products, 6–7, 26–7, 74
  boarding production, 361
  management of, 34–5
  metals, 72
  oil-based products, 143–4
  plastics, 154, 221–2
  recycling, 7
Water, 54, 65–6
  as resource, 3
  energised, 66
  See also Moisture-regulating materials
Waterglass, 212, 393–4
  as pH-regulating surface coat, 435
  paints, 414–15
Wattling, 234, 348–9
Wax, 180, 402, 426
Wedging, stone, 113
Wet-formed walls, 218–19
Windbreaks, 254
Windows, 375–80
  aluminium, 382
  plastic, 382
  sustainable window, 379
  timber, 377–80
Wood, *See* Timber
Wood fibre boards, 285
Wood shavings, 280–2
Wood tar, 157, 176–7, 422, 438–9
Wood vinegar, 176, 439
Woodwool cement, 282–5
Wool, 180, 297–305
  building paper, 298–9
Work satisfaction, 46–8

Zinc, 73, 74, 79
  as climatic material, 259
Zincing, 76–7
Zytan blocks, 270